The Clue Books

TREES

GWEN ALLEN
JOAN DENSLOW

drawings by
TIM HALLIDAY

photographs by
MAURICE NIMMO

OXFORD
UNIVERSITY
PRESS

Oxford University Press, Walton Street, Oxford OX2 6DP

OXFORD NEW YORK TORONTO
DELHI BOMBAY CALCUTTA MADRAS KARACHI
PETALING JAYA SINGAPORE HONG KONG TOKYO
NAIROBI DAR ES SALAAM CAPE TOWN
MELBOURNE AUCKLAND

and associated companies in
BERLIN IBADAN

Oxford is a trade mark of Oxford University Press

© *Oxford University Press 1970*

First published 1970
Reprinted with corrections, 1974, 1976, 1978,
1979, 1982, 1984, 1987, 1990

PRINTED IN HONG KONG

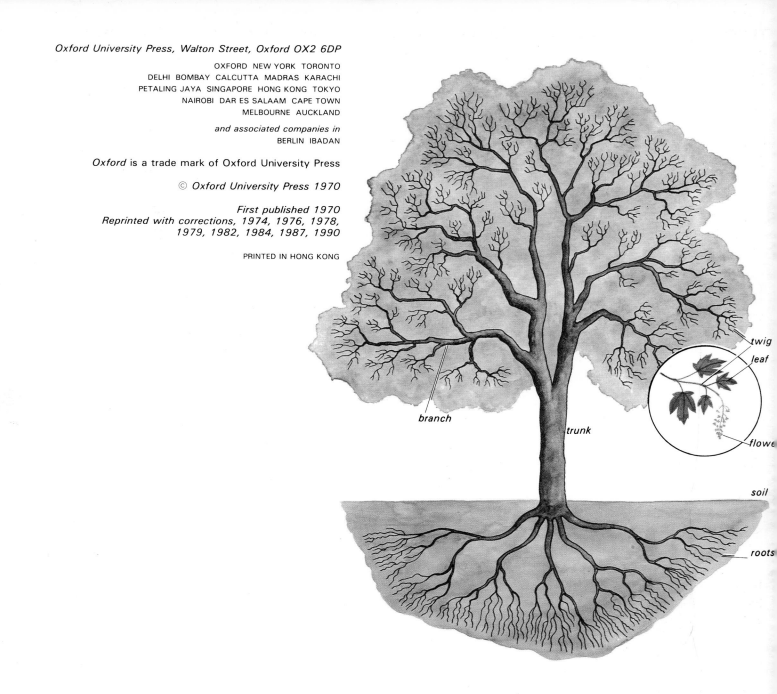

branch

trunk

twig

leaf

flower

soil

roots

TREES are large, woody plants with stems called *trunks*, the smaller stems growing from the trunk are called *branches*. Very small branches are called *twigs*.
Leaves and *flowers* grow from the twigs.
The *roots* of trees spread out under the ground. Some are near the surface; others grow deep into the soil.

Trees that shed all their leaves in winter are called *deciduous*.
Trees that do not shed all their leaves at the same time are called *evergreens*.

In order to find out about and name trees that grow in parks, gardens, orchards, streets or in the countryside you will need to look at them carefully and keep records of what you see.
There are many ways of keeping records.
One way is to make notes and sketches of what you see, in a book. A book like this is called a Field Note Book.

You will find other ways of keeping records on pages 4—8.

Some of these records you will be able to put together to make a book about trees.

If you keep records of the small animals that live on the leaves, in the bark and among the leaf litter of trees, and the birds and furry animals that visit them they will make an interesting addition to your book about trees.

4   If you want to keep records of the winter twigs of deciduous trees (see page 3) you can do this by either drawing, painting, or making plaster casts (see page 6).
You will need to record the exact shape and colour of the buds, the way they are arranged on the twig, and the markings on the twig.

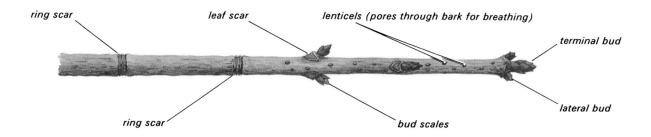

ring scar   leaf scar   lenticels (pores through bark for breathing)   terminal bud

ring scar   bud scales   lateral bud

This twig is 2 years old.
You can tell the age of a twig by counting the number of ring scars.

Take some buds to pieces and using a magnifying lens look at them carefully.

If you want to keep records of the leaves of trees, collect as many different shaped leaves as you can. You can record them by drawing, painting, by sticking pressed leaves and leaf skeletons in your book, or by making leaf prints (page 7) and plaster casts (page 6).
You will need to record the exact shape of the leaf and the arrangement of the veins.

toothed edge   stipules   leaflets

Keep records of the colour of leaves throughout the year.

If you want to keep records of tree flowers, collect as many different kinds of flowers as you can. You can make records by drawing, painting, or pressing the flowers.

You will need to record:

1. The way the flowers are arranged on the stalk

upright clusters

catkins
(tight clusters)

hanging
clusters

2. The exact shape and number of the petals

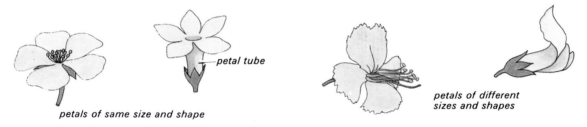

petal tube

petals of same size and shape

petals of different
sizes and shapes

3. Whether the flowers have stamens or ovaries or both in the same flower

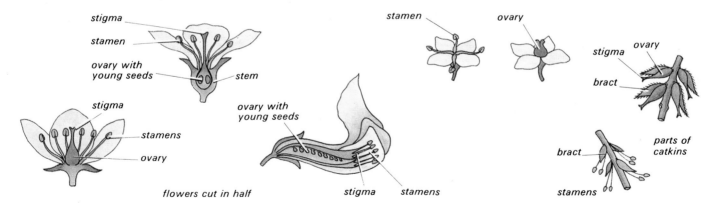

stigma

stamen

ovary with
young seeds

stem

stigma

stamens

ovary

flowers cut in half

stamen

ovary

ovary with
young seeds

stigma

stamens

stigma

ovary

bract

bract

stamens

parts of
catkins

If you want to keep records of the bark of trees you can do this by making scribble prints (page 7) or plaster casts (page 6).

If you want to keep records of *fruits* you can do this by making plaster casts (page 6).

I*

PLASTER CASTS

How to make the MOULDS

You will need soft plasticine or clay, a piece of wood, some paper.

If you are making casts of twigs or fruits, mould the plasticine into a flat shape about 2 cm thick and 3 cm wider and longer than the twig or fruit. Press the specimen carefully into the plasticine until all the important details show. Remove the specimen and keep it in a plastic bag; you will need it again when you paint the cast.

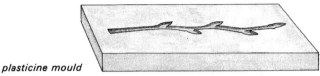

plasticine mould

If you are making bark casts, mould the plasticine into a flat shape about 2 cm thick, 10 cm long and 6 cm wide.
Press the plasticine firmly on to the bark and bang it several times with your fist. Remove the mould carefully.

If you are making leaf casts, mould the plasticine into a flat shape about 2 cm thick and 3 cm wider and longer than the leaf, place a piece of paper on it and press it with a piece of wood until it is really flat. Remove the paper, place the leaf, underside down, on the plasticine, cover it with paper and press firmly with the wood again. Remove the paper and the leaf.

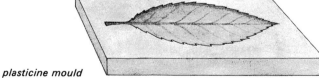

plasticine mould

You will need a small tin, a stick for stirring, some stiff paper, paper clips, plaster of Paris, water paints, clear varnish, and a penknife.

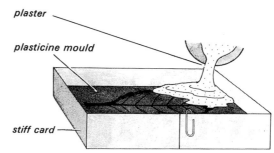

Trim the sides of the plasticine mould to make them straight.
Put a strip of paper 3 cm wide around the plasticine.
Fasten the ends together with a paper clip.
Decide how much plaster is needed to fill the space surrounded by the paper. Put some water into a tin.
Add a little plaster at a time, keeping it well stirred until the mixture is thick but can be poured into the paper ring.
Pour the mixture on to the plasticine and make the top smooth.
Leave until dry, then remove the paper and lever off the plasticine with a penknife.
Paint the cast, copying the details from the real specimens.
Write the name of the tree on the cast.
When dry paint with clear varnish.

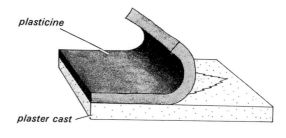

SCRIBBLE PRINTS

You will need some plain paper, wax crayons or coloured pencils with thick centres, water colour paints.
If you are making prints of leaves, place the leaf underside upwards on a flat surface, cover it with a piece of plain paper a little larger than the leaf. Scribble gently over the leaf with a crayon until its shape and markings show clearly.

If you are making prints of bark, place the paper on the trunk of the tree and scribble gently with a black crayon until the markings on the bark show clearly. Paint the waxed side of the paper the colour of the bark.

8   If you want to keep records of tree seedlings, you will need to collect ripe tree fruits and sow them, or find seedlings under trees.

Some seeds germinate if planted from the ripe fruits in autumn, others need a cold spell before they will germinate. After sowing these should be left out of doors over the winter; or the fruits may be kept in a box of damp sand in a cool place during the winter and sown in the spring.

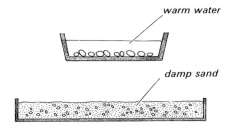

warm water

damp sand

Acorns, chestnuts, and seeds with hard skins should be soaked in warm water for 24 hours before sowing. Read about the tree your seeds come from before you sow them in case they need special treatment.

If you are sowing seeds, you will need clean pots, yogurt or cream cartons or tins with holes in the bottom, small stones (well washed), John Innes compost No. 2 (supplied by garden shops) and plastic bags.

SEED SOWING

1. Put stones and soil in the pot and water it well.

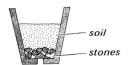

soil

stones

2. Sow one large or a few small seeds in each pot.

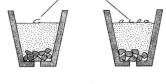

seeds

3. Cover them with a layer of soil equal to their own depth.

4. Put the pot in a plastic bag and close it at the top with wire.

5. Soon after the seeds have germinated open the top of the bag. Keep the soil moist but not wet. Keep in a light place.

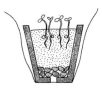

Record in your book about trees what you do and how the plants grow. You may like to make a graph to show how much they grow in height each week. In spring you can also keep records of how quickly tree buds grow.

    If you want to keep records of the heights of trees you will need to make a tree measurer. See *Oxford Junior Mathematics* Book 3, p. 70; or other books about measuring heights. The full grown height of each kind of tree is given on pages 24–62.

Now that you know more about the different parts of trees, you will be able to use the clues on pages 9–24 to find out the name of the tree.
Look carefully at the part of the tree you are using; you will need to use a magnifying lens for the smaller parts and markings. Find the clue that fits it; then you will know where to go for the next clue.

Clue 1.	If you are using leaves	go to clue 2
	If you are using winter twigs	go to clue 26
	If you are using flowers	go to clue 41
	If you are using fruits	go to clue 56

Clue 2.	If the leaves are tough, smooth and shiny	go to clue 3
	If the leaves are very narrow and needlelike	go to clue 6
	If the leaves are not like this	go to clue 10

Clue 3.	If the leaves are lobed and prickly it may be HOLLY	turn to page 32
	If the leaves are not like this	go to clue 4

Clue 4.	If there are many small leaves on the twig it may be YEW	turn to page 63
	If the leaf is more than 3 cm long	go to clue 5

Clue 5.	If the leaf is dark and shiny above but rough underneath it may be HOLM OAK	turn to page 44
	If the leaf is shiny and has a toothed edge it may be a STRAWBERRY TREE	turn to page 57

Clue 6.	If the leaves grow singly on the twig	go to clue 7
	If the leaves grow in clusters on short shoots	go to clue 9

2*

Clue 7. If a small knob or circular scar is left when the leaves fall off

go to clue 8

If the leaves are small, blunt and flattened on the stem it may be CYPRESS

turn to page 62

Clue 8. If the leaves spread out it may be a FIR

turn to page 58

If the leaves curve back towards the stem it may be SPRUCE

turn to page 58

Clue 9. If the leaves are in pairs it may be SCOTS PINE

turn to page 59

If the leaves are in circular clusters it may be CEDAR

turn to page 60

If the young leaves are in tassel-like clusters it may be LARCH

turn to page 61

Clue 10. If the leaf is simple
from
clue 2.

go to clue 11

bud at base of leaf

If the leaf is compound (has several leaflets on the leaf stalk)

go to clue 22

leaflets

bud at base of leaf

Clue 11. If the leaf is lobed

go to clue 12

lobed leaves

If the leaf is not lobed

go to clue 15

Clue 12. If the lobes are pointed and the large veins are arranged like this

go to clue 13

If the lobes are pointed and the large veins are arranged like this

go to clue 14

Clue 12. If the lobes are rounded and the
cont. large veins are arranged like
this it may be OAK

turn to page 44

If the lobes are rounded and the
large veins are arranged like
this it may be MAPLE

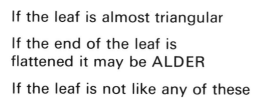

turn to page 27

Clue 13 If the leaf stalk has a cap at the
end that covers the bud it may be PLANE

cap

turn to page 29

If the leaf has white fluff underneath
it may be WHITE POPLAR

turn to page 50

If the leaf is not like either of these it
may be SYCAMORE or NORWAY MAPLE

turn to page 26

Clue 14. If the leaf is sharply lobed and longer
than it is wide it may be TURKEY OAK

turn to page 44

If the leaf is deeply lobed and has leafy
stipules at the base of the leaf stalk
it may be HAWTHORN

stipules

turn to page 36

If the leaf is not like either of these
it may be the SERVICE TREE

turn to page 39

Clue 15. If the leaf is heart-shaped
from
clue 11.

go to clue 16

If the leaf is almost triangular

go to clue 17

If the end of the leaf is
flattened it may be ALDER

turn to page 46

If the leaf is not like any of these

go to clue 18

Clue 16. If the leaf is hairy and has stipules
round the stem it may be MULBERRY

turn to page 40

stipules

If the leaf stalk is covered with red hairs
it may be HAZEL

turn to page 48

If the leaf is delicate and smooth and is
sharply toothed it may be LIME

turn to page 25

If the leaf edge is smooth it may be LILAC

turn to page 55

Clue 17. If the leaf is small and the edge is
double toothed it may be BIRCH

turn to page 47

If the leaf is large and the edge is
almost smooth it may be POPLAR

turn to pages 50–51

Clue 18.
from
clue 15.
If the leaves are long and narrow
have a short stalk and stipules
it may be WILLOW

turn to pages 52–53

stipules

If the leaves are long and
the toothed edge is saw-like
it may be SWEET CHESTNUT

turn to page 45

If the base of the leaf is uneven
it may be ELM

turn to page 41

If the leaf stalk has swellings near
the top, called nectaries, it may be
CHERRY, PLUM, PEACH, or ALMOND

nectaries

turn to pages 33–35

If the leaves are not like any of these

go to clue 19

Clue 19. If the veins go straight to the edge
of the leaf which is doubly
toothed it may be HORNBEAM

turn to page 49

Clue 19.
cont. If the veins go straight to the edge of the leaf which is curved inwards between the veins it may be BEECH

turn to page 43

If the veins curve inwards at the edge of the leaf

go to clue 20

Clue 20. If the back of the leaf is white and hairy

go to clue 21

If the back of the leaf is not hairy and the leaves grow in clusters it may be APPLE

turn to page 37

Clue 21. If the leaf has a short stalk, is pointed, finely toothed and has stipules it may be GOAT WILLOW

stipules

turn to page 52

If the leaf is rounded and double toothed it may be WHITE BEAM

turn to page 39

Clue 22.
from
clue 10. If the leaf is palmate it may be HORSE CHESTNUT

turn to page 28

If the leaf is tri-foliate it may be LABURNUM

turn to page 30

If the leaf is pinnate

go to clue 23

Clue 23. If there are 5 or 7 leaflets it may be ELDER

turn to page 56

or WALNUT

go to clue 24

If there are 7 or more leaflets

go to clue 24

Clue 24. If the leaflets are pale green with smooth edges, have spiny stipules and look like this it may be ROBINIA

stipules

turn to page 31

If the leaflets are dark green, have smooth edges and look like this it may be WALNUT

turn to page 42

If the leaflets are sharply toothed

go to clue 25

Clue 25. If the leaves are arranged in opposite pairs on the twig and the buds are black it may be ASH

turn to page 54

If the leaves are arranged alternately on the twig it may be ROWAN (Mountain Ash)

turn to page 38

Clue 26. from clue 1. If the twig has buds arranged alternately and zig-zags from bud to bud like this

go to clue 27

If the twig has buds arranged in a spiral like this

go to clue 31

If the twig has buds arranged in opposite pairs like this

go to clue 39

If the twig is like this it may be LARCH

turn to page 61

Clue 27. If the buds are oval, often pink and have two bud scales showing, it may be LIME

turn to page 25

If the buds have more than 2 bud scales showing

go to clue 28

Clue 28.

If the buds are rounded go to clue 29

If the buds are long and pointed go to clue 30

Clue 29. If the buds and twig are covered with red hairs it may be HAZEL turn to page 48

If the buds are small and downy it may be ELM turn to page 41

If the buds are large and not like either of these it may be SWEET CHESTNUT turn to page 45

Clue 30. If the bud looks like this it may be BEECH turn to page 43

If the bud curves inwards like this it may be HORNBEAM turn to page 49

Clue 31. If the buds are stalked, purple in colour and have one bud scale it may be ALDER turn to page 46

If the buds are not stalked and are covered with one outer bud scale go to clue 32

If the buds have several bud scales go to clue 33

Clue 32. If the buds lie flat against the stem it may be WILLOW turn to pages 52–53

If the leaf scar forms a ring round the bud it may be PLANE turn to page 29

Clue 33. If the buds are clustered at the end of the twig it may be OAK — turn to page 44

If the buds grow singly on the twig or clustered on short branches — go to clue 34

If the buds are very small — go to clue 35

If the buds are not like any of these — go to clue 36

Clue 34. If the twig and the buds are covered with grey silky hairs it may be LABURNUM or ROWAN — turn to pages 30, 38

If the twigs are red or brown it may belong to the ROSE family — turn to pages 33, 34, 35, 36, 37

Clue 35. If the twig has thorns in pairs by the buds it may be ROBINIA — turn to page 31

If the twig has a single thorn with one or two buds at its base it may be HAWTHORN — turn to page 36

If the twig is very thin and whiplike it may be BIRCH — turn to page 47

Clue 36. If the buds and twigs are covered with white cottony down it may be WHITE POPLAR — turn to page 50

If the buds are shiny and sticky — go to clue 37

If the buds are hairy — go to clue 38

Clue 37. If the twig is smooth and bends easily it may be POPLAR — turn to pages 50–51

If a milky juice appears when the twig is broken it may be MULBERRY — turn to page 40

Clue 38. If the buds are black it may be WALNUT — turn to page 42

If the buds are green it may be WHITE BEAM — turn to page 39

Clue 39.
from
clue 26.

If the buds are black it may be ASH turn to page 54

If the buds are large, brown and sticky
it may be HORSE CHESTNUT turn to page 28

If the buds are green go to clue 40

If the buds are brown, not sticky and the
twigs are hairy it may be MAPLE turn to page 27

If the buds are reddish and the stem is full
of white pith it may be ELDER turn to page 56

Clue 40. If there are 2 buds at the end of the
twig it may be LILAC turn to page 55

If there is one large bud at the
end of the twig it may
be SYCAMORE turn to page 26

Clue 41.
from
clue 1.

If the flowers have large
white or coloured petals
  (see page 5) go to clue 42

If the flowers have small
greenish petals
  (see page 5) go to clue 49

If the flowers have no petals and
they are arranged in catkins
  (see page 5) go to clue 50

parts of catkins

Clue 42. If the petals are all the
same shape and size go to clue 43

If the petals are different
shapes and sizes go to clue 47

4*

Clue 43. If the petals are all separate

go to clue 44

If the petals are joined together

go to clue 45

Clue 44. If the flowers have 5 petals and the ovaries are inside the petals it may be CHERRY, PLUM, ALMOND, or PEACH

half flower

turn to pages 33–35

If the flowers have 5 petals and the ovaries are inside the stem below the petals it may be HAWTHORN, APPLE, ROWAN, or WHITE BEAM

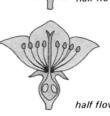

half flower

turn to pages 36–39

Clue 45. If the flower is bell-shaped it may be a STRAWBERRY TREE

turn to page 57

If the flower has 4 white, mauve, or purple petals joined to make a long tube it may be LILAC

turn to page 55

If the flower has creamy white petals joined to make a short tube

go to clue 46

Clue 46. If there are 5 petals it may be ELDER

turn to page 56

If there are 4 petals it may be HOLLY

turn to page 32

Clue 47. **from clue 42** If the flowers look like this

go to clue 48

If the flowers look like this it may be HORSE CHESTNUT

turn to page 28

Clue 48. If the flowers are yellow it may be LABURNUM turn to page 30

If the flowers are white or pink it may be ROBINIA turn to page 31

Clue 49.
from
clue 41
If there are many flowers
hanging in clusters
it may be SYCAMORE turn to page 26

If there are a few flowers
in an upright cluster
it may be MAPLE turn to page 27

If the flower hangs from
a long bract it
may be LIME turn to page 25

—bract

Clue 50.
from
clue 41.
If the tree blooms before the leaves grow go to clue 51

If the tree blooms when it is in leaf go to clue 54

Clue 51. If the flowers that have
stamens are in long
hanging clusters go to clue 52

If the flowers that have
ovaries grow in long
hanging clusters it
may be POPLAR or WILLOW turn to pages 50–53

If the flowers grow in
upright clusters go to clue 53

20

Clue 52. If the flowers that have ovaries grow on
the same tree and look like this
it may be HAZEL

turn to page 48

If the flowers that have ovaries grow on
the same tree and look like this
it may be ALDER

turn to page 46

If there are no flowers with ovaries on
the tree it may be POPLAR

turn to pages 50–51

Clue 53. If the flowers are pink and the tree
blooms in February it may be ELM

turn to page 41

If the flowers are dark purple and the
tree blooms in April or May
it may be ASH

turn to page 54

If the flowers are yellow or green
it may be WILLOW

turn to pages 52–53

Clue 54. If the catkins are long and look
like this it may be
BIRCH or HORNBEAM

turn to pages 47, 49

If the catkins are round and look
like this it
may be PLANE

turn to page 29

Clue 54.
cont. If the catkins are short and thick and they all look like this it may be MULBERRY

turn to page 40

If the flowers are in long scented clusters and the tree blooms in July it may be SWEET CHESTNUT

turn to page 45

If the flowers are not like any of these

go to clue 55

Clue 55. If the flowers look like this it may be OAK

stigmas

stamens

turn to page 44

If the flowers look like this it may be WALNUT

ovaries

stamens

turn to page 42

If the flowers look like this it may be BEECH

stigmas

stamens

turn to page 43

Clue 56.
from
clue 1. If the fruit is soft and juicy when ripe

go to clue 57

If the fruit is brittle and dry when ripe

go to clue 60

Clue 57. If the dead flower can be seen on the top of the fruit it may be ROWAN, APPLE, HAWTHORN or WHITE BEAM

turn to pages 36–39

If the fruit is not like this

go to clue 58

Clue 58. If the fruit looks like a strawberry it may be a STRAWBERRY TREE

turn to page 57

If there are many black fruits it may be ELDER

turn to page 56

If the fruits are red or black and grow in tight clusters it may be MULBERRY

turn to page 40

If the fruits are small, smooth and red it may be HOLLY

turn to page 32

If the fruits are large and have one large stone it may be PLUM, PEACH, or CHERRY

turn to pages 33–35

If the fruit splits open

go to clue 59

Clue 59. If the fruit is green and prickly it may be HORSE CHESTNUT

turn to page 28

If the fruit is smooth and has a flattened nut it may be ALMOND

turn to page 35

If the fruit is smooth and has a round nut it may be WALNUT

turn to page 42

Clue 60. from clue 56.

If the fruit is a woody cone

go to clue 61

If the fruit bursts to shed the ripe seeds

go to clue 66

If the fruit falls with the seed inside it

go to clue 67

Clue 61. If the scales overlap at the edges   go to clue 62

If the scales do not overlap   go to clue 63

Clue 62. If the whole cone falls off the tree   go to clue 64

If the cone breaks up on the tree and
the scales fall to the ground   go to clue 65

Clue 63. If the tree is evergreen it may be CYPRESS   turn to page 62

If the tree is not evergreen it may be ALDER   turn to page 46

Clue 64. If the scales have a notch at the end
it may be PINE   turn to page 59

If the scales are not notched and the cones
are less than 3 cm long it may be LARCH   turn to page 61

If the scales are not notched and the cones
are longer than 3 cm it may be SPRUCE   turn to page 58

Clue 65. If the cones are flattened at
both ends it may be CEDAR   turn to page 60

If the cones are long it may be a FIR   turn to page 58

Clue 66.
from
clue 60.

If the fruit is a pod it
may be LABURNUM or ROBINIA   turn to pages 30–31

If the fruit looks like this
it may be WILLOW or POPLAR   turn to pages 50–53

If the fruit looks like this
it may be LILAC   turn to page 55

Clue 67.   If the fruits are hairy
from   it may be PLANE turn to page 29
clue 60.

   If the fruits have wings go to clue 68

   If the fruits are not like any of these go to clue 69

Clue 68. If the fruits look like one of these turn to the page shown.

LIME page 25   ELM page 41   ASH page 54   HORNBEAM page 49

enlarged

MAPLE page 27   SYCAMORE page 26   BIRCH page 47   ALDER page 46

Clue 69. If the fruits look like one of these turn to the page shown.

HAZEL page 48   OAK page 44   SWEET CHESTNUT page 45   BEECH page 43

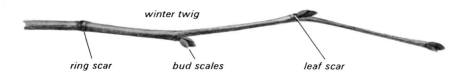

winter twig

ring scar   bud scales   leaf scar

Lime or Linden trees grow in parks and streets. They bloom in July, and have strongly scented flowers which attract bees. During the summer large numbers of aphids live on the leaves; they produce a sticky substance called 'honeydew', which may fall from the trees and make the ground underneath sticky too. Deer and cattle eat the leaves and young shoots, and so do caterpillars of the Lime Hawk Moth.

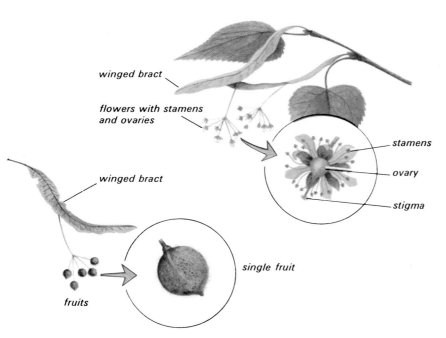

winged bract

flowers with stamens and ovaries

winged bract

stamens

ovary

stigma

fruits

single fruit

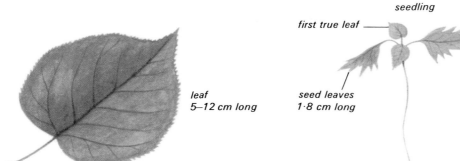

leaf
5–12 cm long

seedling

first true leaf

seed leaves
1·8 cm long

Lime in summer

Scale : 1 cm represents 3 metres

cm

SYCAMORE or GREAT MAPLE
(Aceraceae)

Sycamore trees are most common in woods
and hedges; many seedlings may be found
there in the spring. Squirrels sometimes eat
the fruits and bark of the tree. The leaves
may become covered with a sugary sap. The
trunk of its relative the Sugar Maple is tapped
and Maple sugar is collected.

The leaves of the Norway Maple are like
Sycamore leaves in shape but are yellow
green in colour; they turn a deep yellow in
the autumn.

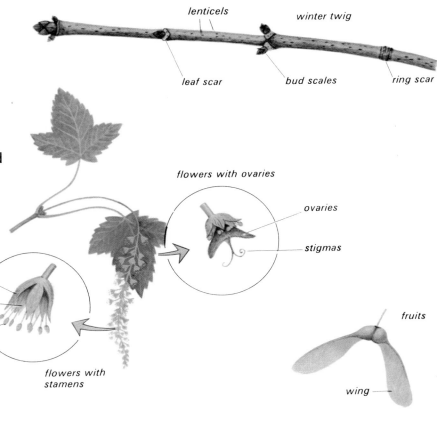

lenticels

winter twig

leaf scar

bud scales

ring scar

flowers with ovaries

ovaries

stigmas

sepals

petals

stamens

flowers with stamens

fruits

wing

cm

Sycamore in summer

Scale: 1 cm represents 3 metres

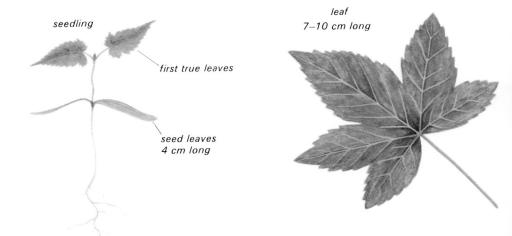

seedling

first true leaves

*seed leaves
4 cm long*

*leaf
7–10 cm long*

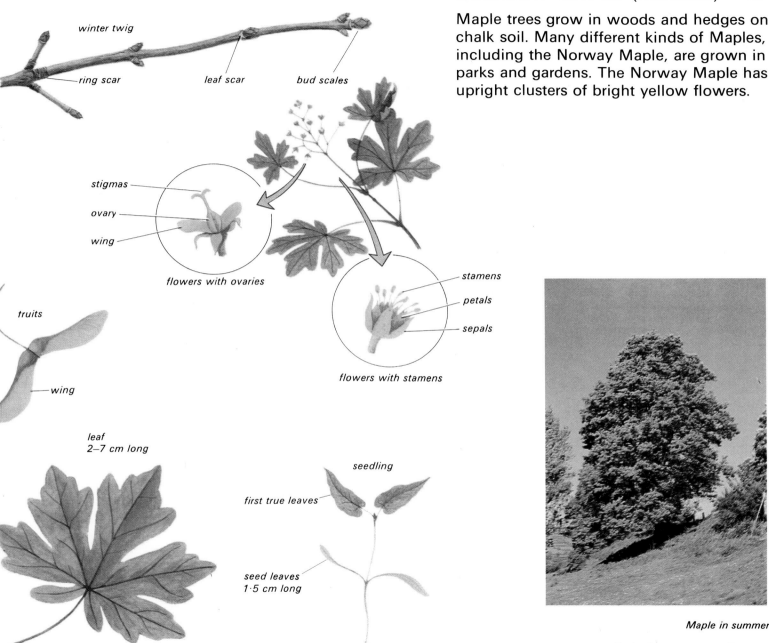

winter twig

ring scar   leaf scar   bud scales

COMMON MAPLE (*Aceraceae*)   27

Maple trees grow in woods and hedges on chalk soil. Many different kinds of Maples, including the Norway Maple, are grown in parks and gardens. The Norway Maple has upright clusters of bright yellow flowers.

stigmas

ovary

wing

flowers with ovaries

stamens

petals

sepals

flowers with stamens

fruits

wing

leaf
2–7 cm long

seedling

first true leaves

seed leaves
1·5 cm long

Maple in summer

Scale : 1 cm represents 3 metres

cm

28 HORSE CHESTNUT
(*Hippocastanaceae*)

Horse Chestnut trees are often planted in parks and streets. The flowers are either white or dark pink and bloom in spring; the stamens produce red pollen. The seeds, called conkers, are eaten by cattle but not by horses.

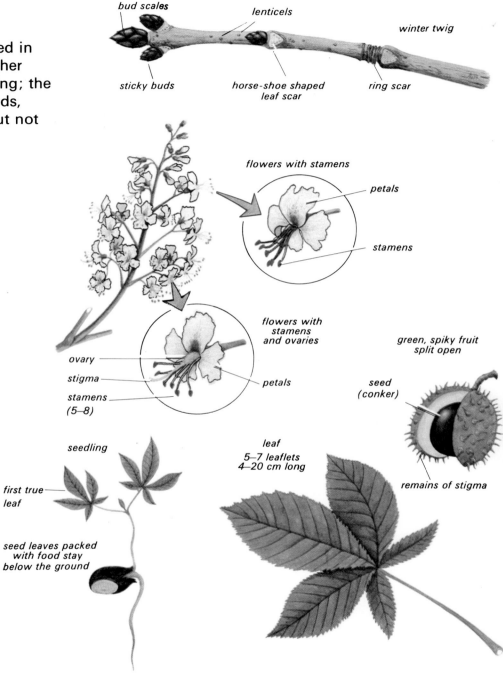

bud scales

lenticels

winter twig

sticky buds

horse-shoe shaped leaf scar

ring scar

flowers with stamens

petals

stamens

flowers with stamens and ovaries

ovary

stigma

stamens (5–8)

petals

green, spiky fruit split open

seed (conker)

remains of stigma

seedling

first true leaf

seed leaves packed with food stay below the ground

leaf
5–7 leaflets
4–20 cm long

cm

Horse Chestnut in spring

Scale: 1 cm represents 3 metres

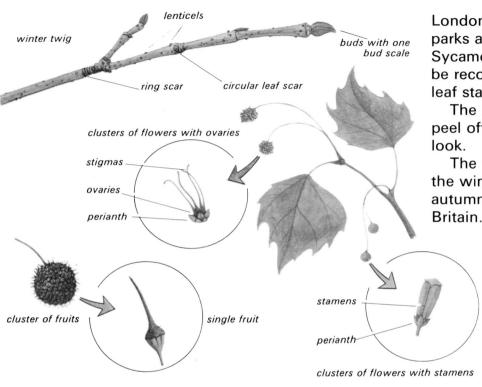

winter twig

lenticels

buds with one
bud scale

ring scar

circular leaf scar

clusters of flowers with ovaries

stigmas

ovaries

perianth

cluster of fruits

single fruit

stamens

perianth

clusters of flowers with stamens

London Plane trees are most often planted in parks and streets. The leaves are very like Sycamore or Norway Maple leaves, but can be recognized by the cap at the end of the leaf stalk.

The bark is smooth and the outer layers peel off in patches giving the trunk a piebald look.

The fruit balls hang on the tree through the winter. Twigs will root if planted in the autumn, but seeds rarely germinate in Britain.

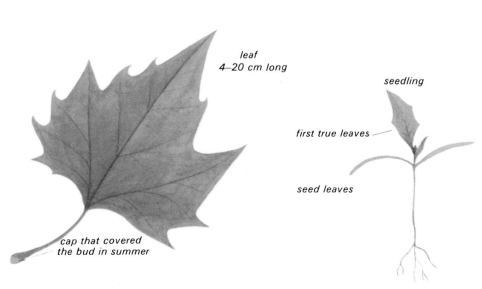

leaf
4–20 cm long

seedling

first true leaves

seed leaves

cap that covered
the bud in summer

cm

London Plane in spring

Scale : 1 cm represents 3 metres

Laburnum trees are grown in parks and gardens. The leaflets close together at night and spread out during the daytime. Flowers bloom in May or June and are visited by Humblebees. Old fruit pods hang on the trees all through the winter.

The black seeds are poisonous.

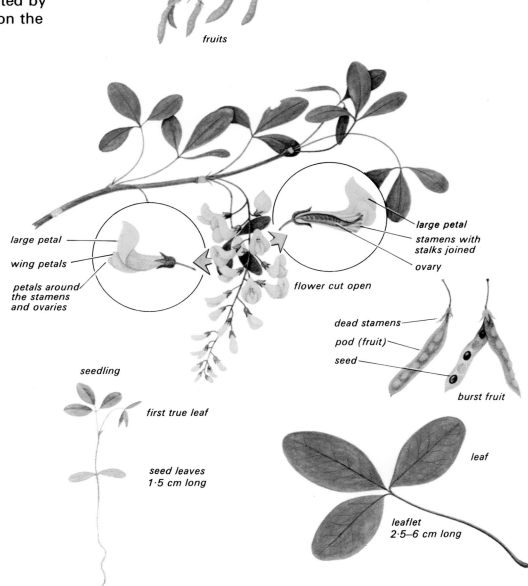

winter twig

very small buds

leaf scars

ring scar

fruits

large petal

wing petals

petals around the stamens and ovaries

large petal

stamens with stalks joined

ovary

flower cut open

dead stamens

pod (fruit)

seed

burst fruit

seedling

first true leaf

seed leaves 1·5 cm long

leaf

leaflet 2·5–6 cm long

cm

Laburnum in early summer

Scale : 1 cm represents 3 metres

False Acacia

Robinia trees are planted in parks and streets; they are named after Robin, a seventeenth century Parisian gardener.

The trees have fluted trunks with a spiral twist.

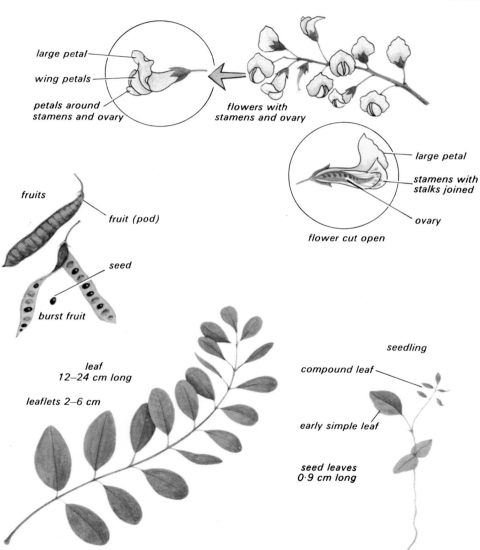

winter twig

ring scar   spiny stipules   leaf scar   very small bud

large petal

wing petals

petals around
stamens and ovary

flowers with
stamens and ovary

large petal

stamens with
stalks joined

ovary

flower cut open

fruits

fruit (pod)

seed

burst fruit

leaf
12–24 cm long

leaflets 2–6 cm

seedling

compound leaf

early simple leaf

seed leaves
0·9 cm long

Robinia in spring

Scale : 1 cm represents 3 metres

cm

Holly trees grow in woods, hedgerows, parks, and gardens. In spring, flowers containing ovaries which ripen to produce the red berries are found on some trees. On other trees are flowers with stamens that make pollen.

Trees with stamen flowers never produce berries. Honey bees visit the flowers to gather nectar and the seeds in the bird's droppings fall to the ground away from the tree and may germinate there.

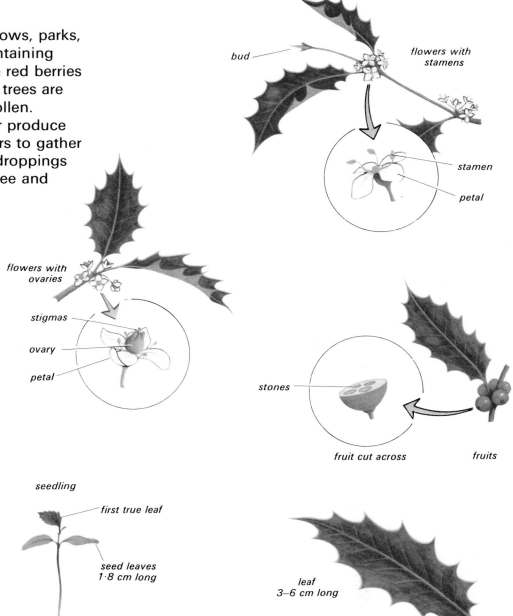

bud

flowers with stamens

stamen

petal

flowers with ovaries

stigmas

ovary

petal

stones

fruit cut across

fruits

Holly in winter

Scale : 1 cm represents 3 metres

cm

seedling

first true leaf

seed leaves
1·8 cm long

leaf
3–6 cm long

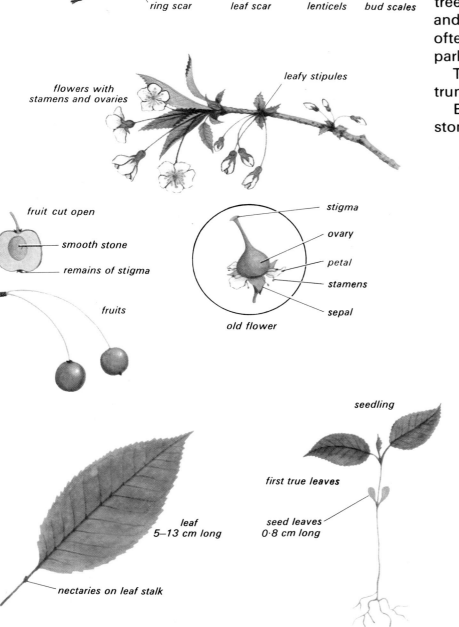

winter twig

ring scar   leaf scar   lenticels   bud scales

flowers with
stamens and ovaries

leafy stipules

fruit cut open

smooth stone

remains of stigma

fruits

stigma

ovary

petal

stamens

sepal

old flower

leaf
5–13 cm long

nectaries on leaf stalk

seedling

first true leaves

seed leaves
0·8 cm long

Wild cherries grow in woods and hedges; trees with edible fruit are planted in gardens and orchards. Ornamental Japanese cherries, often with double flowers, are planted in parks and streets.

The bark peels off in thin strips round the trunk.

Birds eat the fruits, sometimes leaving the stones hanging from the tree.

cm

Cherry tree in spring

Scale: 1 cm represents 3 metres

Plum trees grow wild in hedges but are more often planted in gardens and orchards. There are several kinds including the Greengage, Apricot, and wild Bullace (which may be thorny).

Prunes are dried plums.

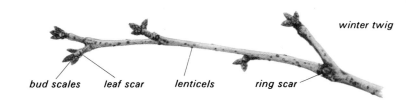

winter twig

bud scales   leaf scar   lenticels   ring scar

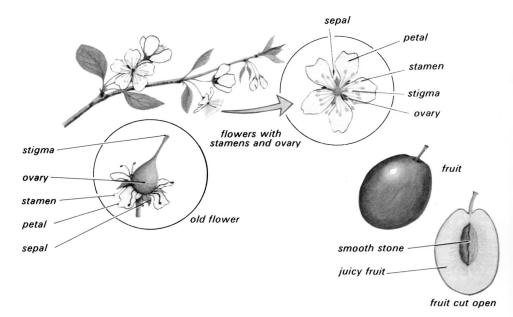

sepal
petal
stamen
stigma
ovary

flowers with stamens and ovary

stigma
ovary
stamen
petal
sepal

old flower

Plum tree in spring

Scale : 1 cm represents 3 metres

cm

fruit

smooth stone
juicy fruit

fruit cut open

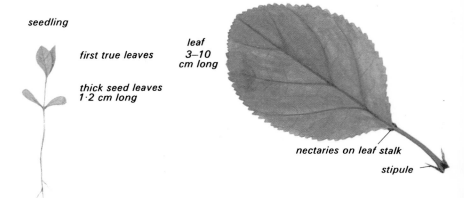

seedling

first true leaves

thick seed leaves
1·2 cm long

leaf
3–10
cm long

nectaries on leaf stalk

stipule

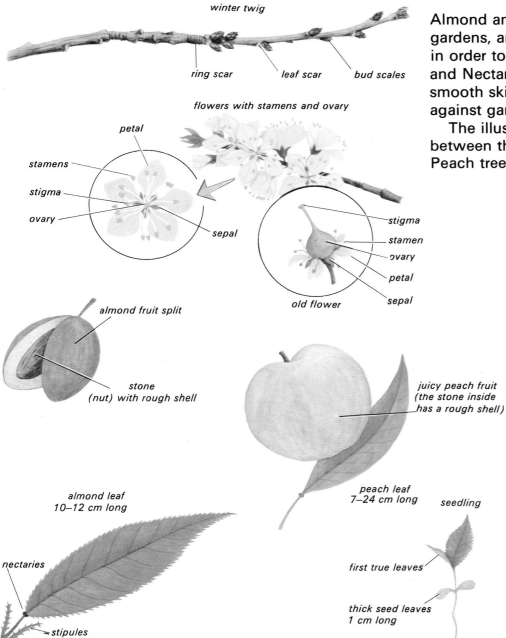

winter twig

ring scar   leaf scar   bud scales

flowers with stamens and ovary

petal

stamens

stigma

ovary

sepal

stigma

stamen

ovary

petal

old flower

sepal

almond fruit split

stone
(nut) with rough shell

juicy peach fruit
(the stone inside
has a rough shell)

almond leaf
10–12 cm long

peach leaf
7–24 cm long

seedling

first true leaves

thick seed leaves
1 cm long

nectaries

stipules

Almond and Peach trees are planted in parks, gardens, and streets as ornamental trees, but in order to produce good ripe fruit Peaches and Nectarines (a kind of peach with a smooth skin) are grown in greenhouses, or against garden walls in protected places.

The illustrations show the differences between the leaves and fruits of Almond and Peach trees.

cm

Almond tree in spring

Scale : 1 cm represents 3 metres

Hawthorn trees are very common in woods and hedges. They have been used for hedging ever since land was enclosed. Ornamental trees with large flowers and fruits are planted in parks, gardens, and streets.

Animals eat the leaves of hawthorn trees, but the tree and the seedlings are protected by thorns.

The strongly scented flowers which bloom in May or June attract flies, beetles, and other insects.

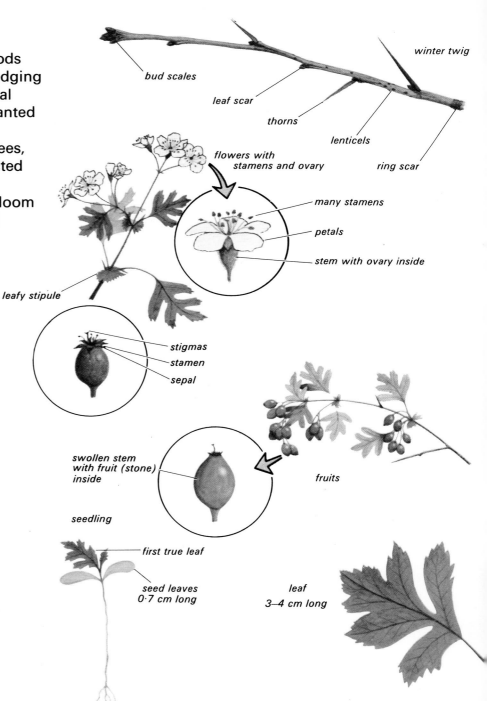

winter twig

bud scales

leaf scar

thorns

lenticels

ring scar

flowers with
stamens and ovary

many stamens

petals

stem with ovary inside

leafy stipule

stigmas
stamen
sepal

swollen stem
with fruit (stone)
inside

fruits

seedling

first true leaf

seed leaves
0·7 cm long

leaf
3–4 cm long

Hawthorn in spring

cm

Scale : 1 cm represents 3 metres

winter twig

lenticel

bud scales

short shoot   leaf scar

ring scar

flowers with stamens
and ovary

stigmas

stamen

petal

old flower

stamen

sepal

petal

swollen stem with
the fruit (core) inside

fruit

dead sepals and stamens

seedling

first true leaf

leaf
3–5 cm long

seed leaves
1–2 cm long

stipule

Varieties of trees called Flowering Crabs, with large flowers and often red leaves are grown in parks and streets. Wild Crab Apple trees grow in woods and hedges; the fruit is very sour, but pigs will eat them.

Trees that produce fruit that is good to eat are grown in gardens and orchards. Some of the fruit is sweet; others are sour and need cooking.

Some apples grown in orchards are used for making cider.

Many insects live in apple trees. Mistletoe often grows on old trees.

cm

Flowering Crab Apple in spring

Scale: 1 cm represents 3 metres

38   ROWAN (*Rosaceae*)

Rowan trees grow wild in woods and on mountain sides; they are planted in parks, gardens, and streets. The trunks have dark bands of lenticels round them.

The wood is sometimes used for making archers' bows.

Blackbirds eat the scarlet berries.

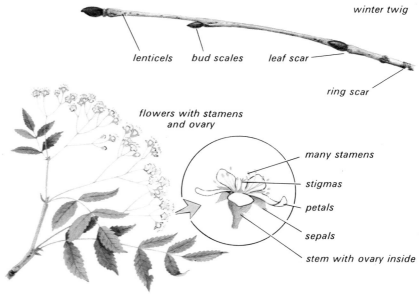

winter twig

lenticels   bud scales   leaf scar

ring scar

flowers with stamens and ovary

many stamens

stigmas

petals

sepals

stem with ovary inside

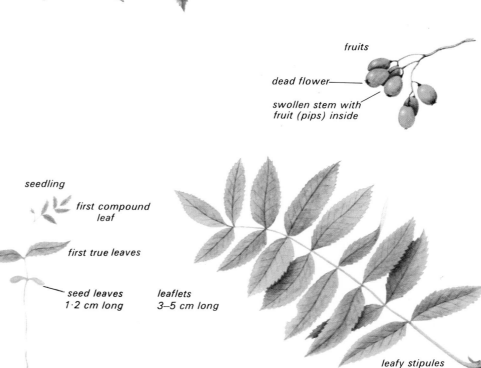

fruits

dead flower

swollen stem with fruit (pips) inside

seedling

first compound leaf

first true leaves

seed leaves 1·2 cm long

leaflets 3–5 cm long

leafy stipules

Rowan in summer

cm

Scale : 1 cm represents 3 metres

Whitebeam trees grow on chalk or limestone hills. Trees growing in woods look very white among the other trees.

Several kinds of Whitebeam trees, with different shaped leaves, are planted in parks and streets.

The tree with pointed, lobed leaves is called the Service Tree.

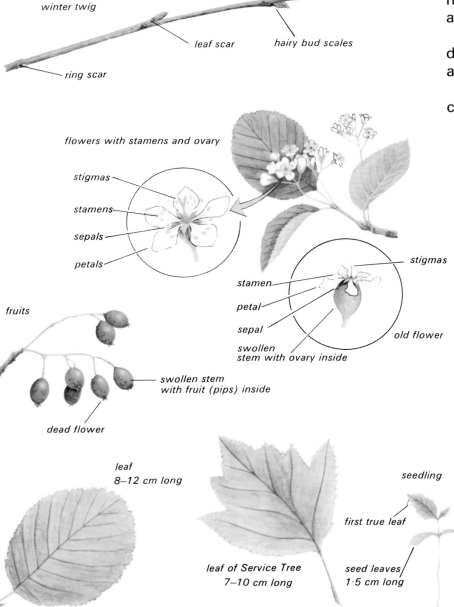

winter twig

leaf scar

hairy bud scales

ring scar

flowers with stamens and ovary

stigmas

stamens

sepals

petals

stigmas

stamen

petal

sepal

old flower

swollen stem with ovary inside

fruits

swollen stem with fruit (pips) inside

dead flower

leaf 8–12 cm long

leaf of Service Tree 7–10 cm long

seedling

first true leaf

seed leaves 1·5 cm long

stipule

cm

Whitebeam in early summer

Scale : 1 cm represents 3 metres

40 MULBERRY (*Moraceae*)

Mulberry trees are grown in gardens; the leaves are the favourite food of silk worms.

The ripe fruit is delicious to eat raw or in pies.

Blackbirds and starlings take the fruit off the trees.

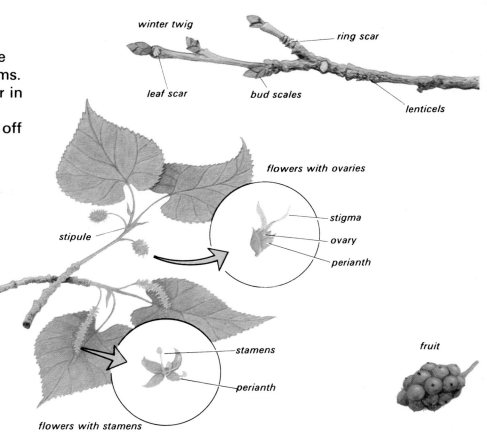

winter twig

ring scar

leaf scar

bud scales

lenticels

flowers with ovaries

stipule

stigma

ovary

perianth

stamens

perianth

flowers with stamens

fruit

cm

Mulberry in spring

Scale : 1 cm represents 3 metres

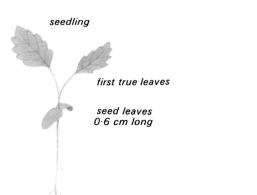

seedling

first true leaves

seed leaves
0·6 cm long

leaf
5–10 cm long

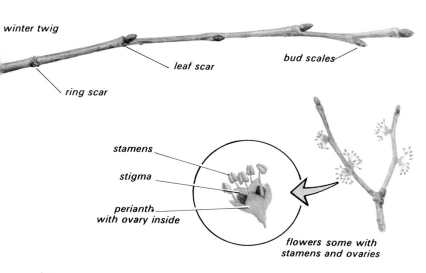

winter twig

leaf scar

ring scar

bud scales

stamens

stigma

perianth with ovary inside

flowers some with stamens and ovaries

Elm trees grow in hedges and in parks. In spring, the branches look pink and fluffy when the trees are blooming.

Caterpillars of Large Tortoiseshell butterflies feed on the leaves.

The seeds of the Wych Elm germinate much more easily than the seeds of the Common Elm.

The illustrations show the difference between the leaves and fruits of Common and Wych Elm trees.

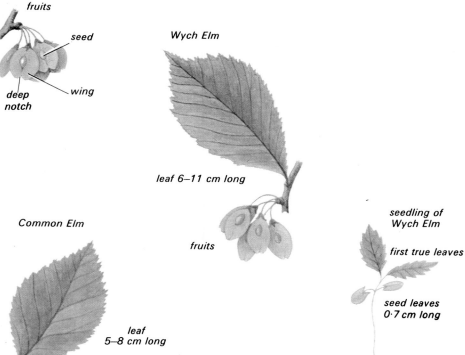

fruits

seed

deep notch

wing

Wych Elm

leaf 6–11 cm long

Common Elm

fruits

leaf 5–8 cm long

seedling of Wych Elm

first true leaves

seed leaves 0·7 cm long

cm

Common Elm in summer

Scale : 1 cm represents 3 metres

42 WALNUT (*Juglandaceae*)

Walnut trees are planted in parks and fields. The unripe fruits can be pickled whole. When the fruits ripen the walnuts fall out. Squirrels and rooks eat the nuts. The leaves have a strong spicy smell when crushed.

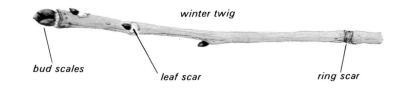

winter twig

bud scales

leaf scar

ring scar

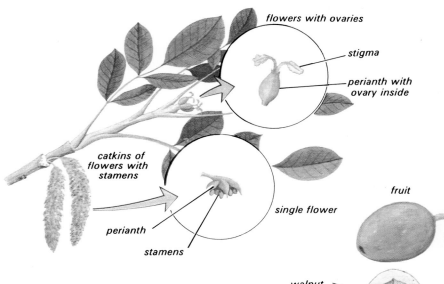

flowers with ovaries

stigma

perianth with ovary inside

catkins of flowers with stamens

single flower

perianth

stamens

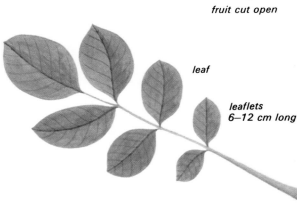

fruit

walnut

outer coat

fruit cut open

cm

Walnut in summer

Scale: 1 cm represents 3 metres

seedling

first very small leaves

burst fruit with seed leaves inside

leaf

leaflets 6–12 cm long

Beech trees grow in woods. In summer the leaves are so thickly spread that it is very dark and shady underneath, and few plants can grow there.

Deer, mice, squirrels, and badgers eat the mast.

Sometimes shrivelled leaves hang on the tree until the following spring.

The Copper Beech tree with larger red leaves is often grown in parks.

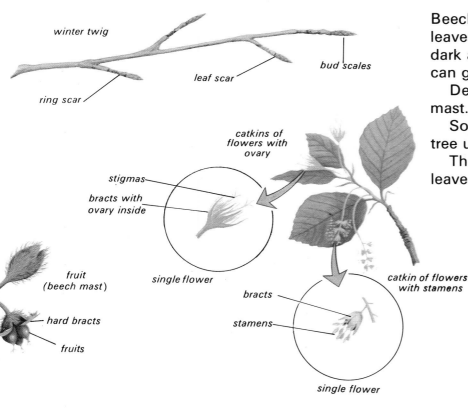

winter twig

ring scar

leaf scar

bud scales

catkins of flowers with ovary

stigmas

bracts with ovary inside

single flower

fruit (beech mast)

hard bracts

fruits

bracts

stamens

catkin of flowers with stamens

single flower

Copper Beech leaf 8–11cm long

leaf 4–8 cm long

seedling

first true leaves

seed leaves

cm

Beech in summer

Scale : 1 cm represents 3 metres

Oak trees grow in woods, hedgerows, and parks.

Jays and pigeons eat the acorns; squirrels peel them and eat the seeds or store them for winter food by burying them. Stag beetles eat the leaves, and their larvae (young) live and feed on old, dead wood. Oak apples and other galls grow round the eggs of insects laid in the Oak buds; caterpillars and many other insects live in the leaves, flowers, fruit, and bark.

The illustrations show the different shaped leaves of Turkey and Holm Oaks.

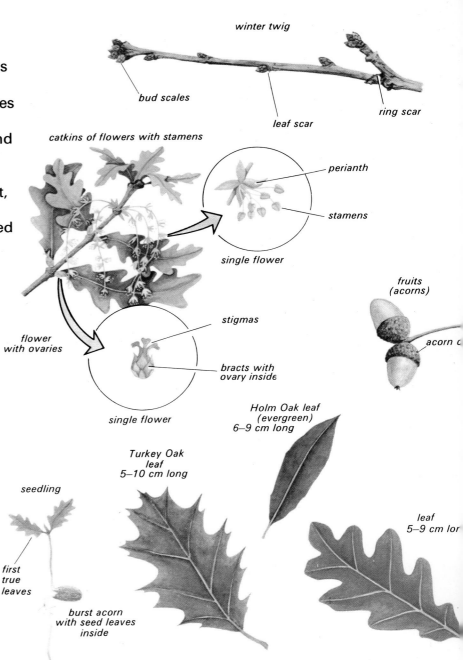

winter twig

bud scales

leaf scar

ring scar

catkins of flowers with stamens

perianth

stamens

single flower

flower
with ovaries

stigmas

bracts with
ovary inside

single flower

fruits
(acorns)

acorn c

Holm Oak leaf
(evergreen)
6–9 cm long

Turkey Oak
leaf
5–10 cm long

seedling

first
true
leaves

burst acorn
with seed leaves
inside

leaf
5–9 cm lor

Oak in summer

Scale: 1 cm represents 3 metres

cm

Sweet Chestnut trees grow in woods and parks. The flowers bloom in July and have a strong smell.

Nuts from trees grown in Britain are small; squirrels and mice eat them.

Large Chestnuts which we roast in autumn come from trees grown in warmer countries.

The bark on the trunk of the tree has a spiral twist.

winter twig

ring scar

leaf scar

bud scales

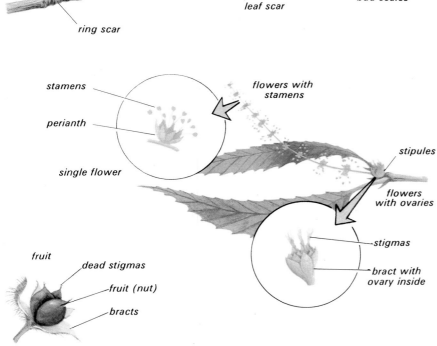

stamens

perianth

single flower

flowers with stamens

stipules

flowers with ovaries

stigmas

bract with ovary inside

fruit

dead stigmas

fruit (nut)

bracts

leaf 7–14 cm long

seedling

first true leaves

burst nut with seed leaves inside

cm

Sweet Chestnut in summer

Scale: 1 cm represents 3 metres

Alder trees most often grow by rivers or in other damp places; sometimes in mountain bogs.

The fruit is easily carried by water because the tiny wings are filled with air.

winter twig

bud scale

old fruit

stalked bud

lenticels

leaf scar

ring scar

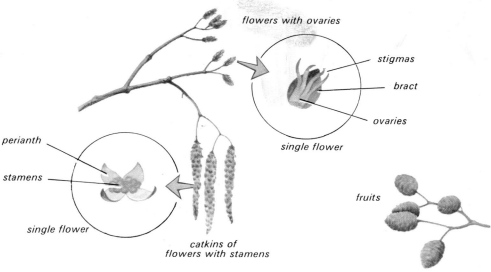

flowers with ovaries

stigmas

bract

ovaries

single flower

perianth

stamens

single flower

catkins of
flowers with stamens

fruits

cm

Alders in winter

Scale: 1 cm represents 3 metres

seedling

first true leaves

seed leaves
0·7 cm long

leaf
5–9 cm long

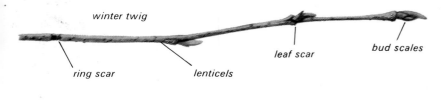

winter twig

ring scar

lenticels

leaf scar

bud scales

Birch trees grow in gardens, parks, and wild in many parts of the country. The bark of the Silver Birch is silvery and peels off in fine shreds.

The flexible twigs are used to make garden brooms; and whips used to be made of the thin branches.

The tangled masses of twigs that look like birds' nests are caused by a tiny spider-like animal. Birch seeds need light in order to germinate; they should be scattered on the surface of damp soil.

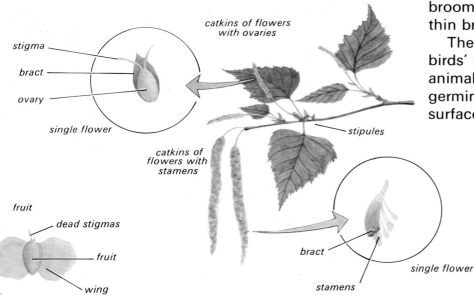

catkins of flowers with ovaries

stigma

bract

ovary

single flower

catkins of flowers with stamens

stipules

bract

single flower

stamens

fruit

dead stigmas

fruit

wing

Silver Birch in spring

Scale : 1 cm represents 3 metres

cm

seedling

first true leaves

seed leaves
0·4 cm long

leaf
3—4 cm long

Hazel trees grow in woods and hedges; they are cultivated in Kent for their nuts (Kent cobs). Hazel sticks are used for making hurdles.

The nuts are attacked by weevils which bore a small hole in the shell and lay their eggs inside. When the eggs hatch the grubs eat the seed.

Squirrels eat or bury the good nuts.

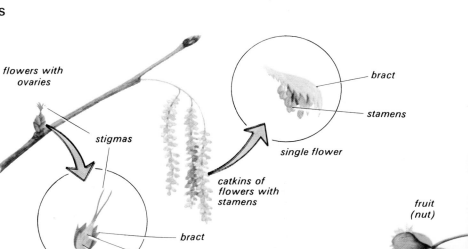

winter twig

bud scales

leaf scar

ring scar

flowers with ovaries

stigmas

bract

stamens

single flower

catkins of flowers with stamens

bract

ovary

single flower

perianth

fruit (nut)

bracts

dead stigma

Hazel in summer

cm

Scale: 1 cm represents 3 metres

seedling

first true leaf

burst fruit with seed leaves inside

leaf 7–11 cm long

reddish hairs

winter twig

ring scar

leaf scar

bud scales

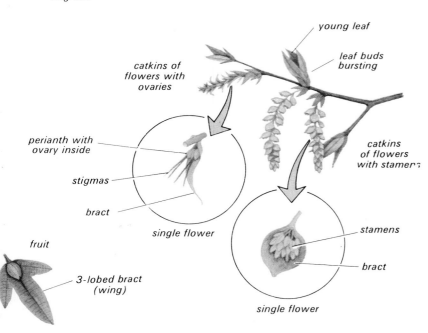

young leaf

leaf buds bursting

catkins of flowers with ovaries

perianth with ovary inside

stigmas

bract

single flower

catkins of flowers with stamens

stamens

bract

single flower

fruit

3-lobed bract (wing)

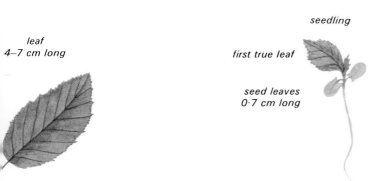

leaf
4–7 cm long

seedling

first true leaf

seed leaves
0.7 cm long

Hornbeam trees grow in woods, hedges, and in parks.

The very hard wood was once used to make yokes for oxen. It is said that because the beam of wood was attached to the horns of the oxen the tree was called Hornbeam.

Because the wood burns slowly and with a very hot flame it makes good charcoal.

cm

Hornbeam in spring

Scale : 1 cm represents 3 metres

50 WHITE POPLAR and ASPEN
(*Salicaceae*)

Aspen trees grow in woods; White Poplars are planted in parks or damp meadows. The leaves of Poplars, especially the Aspen, tremble in the wind because their leaf stalks are flattened.

The wood is used for making chip baskets, matches, and match boxes.

Goat Moth caterpillars live inside the branches and eat the wood around them; many other caterpillars including those of the Poplar Hawk Moth eat the leaves.

The illustrations show the difference between the leaves of the White Poplar and Aspen trees.

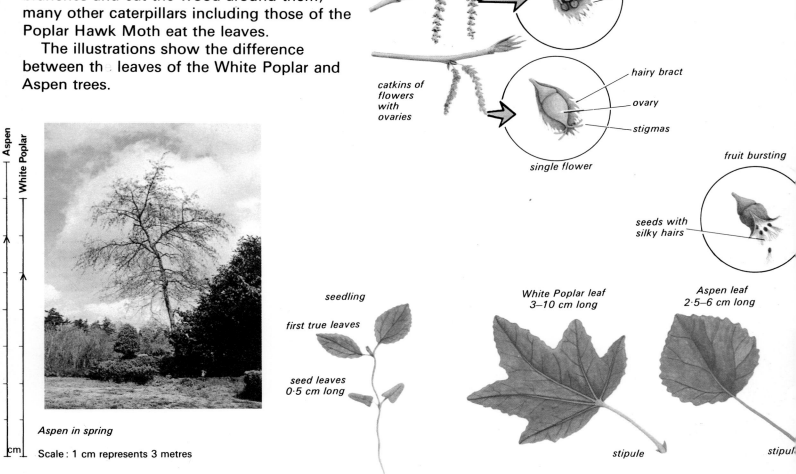

winter twig

bud scales

leaf scar

lenticels

ring scar

catkins of flowers with stamens

single flower

stamens

hairy bract

catkins of flowers with ovaries

hairy bract

ovary

stigmas

single flower

fruit bursting

seeds with silky hairs

Aspen

White Poplar

Aspen in spring

Scale: 1 cm represents 3 metres

seedling

first true leaves

seed leaves 0·5 cm long

White Poplar leaf 3–10 cm long

Aspen leaf 2·5–6 cm long

stipule

stipule

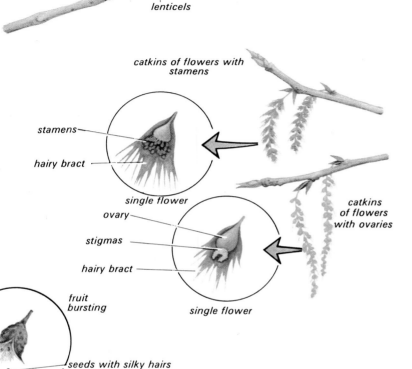

winter twig

ring scar

leaf scar

bud scale

lenticels

catkins of flowers with stamens

stamens

hairy bract

single flower

ovary

stigmas

hairy bract

catkins of flowers with ovaries

single flower

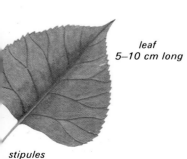

fruit bursting

seeds with silky hairs

leaf 5–10 cm long

stipules

seedling

seed leaves 0·5 cm long

Black Poplar trees grow well in smoky towns; they are similar in shape to White Poplar trees but their leaves are like those of the Lombardy Poplar, which grows tall quickly, and is often planted to hide dumps and factories.

Poplar twigs root easily in water. When the roots are well grown the twigs may be planted in pots of soil or in the garden.

Lombardy Poplar

Black Poplar

Lombardy Poplar in summer

Scale: 1 cm represents 3 metres   cm

Osiers grow by streams, ponds, and in marshes. In Osier beds the new wood is cut back each year and used for making baskets and lobster pots. The head of new branches is called a pollard.

Goat (Palm or Pussy) Willow trees grow in woods and hedges. The tree blooms very early in the spring; the flowers are visited by bees and moths.

The illustrations show the difference between the leaves of Osier and Goat Willow trees.

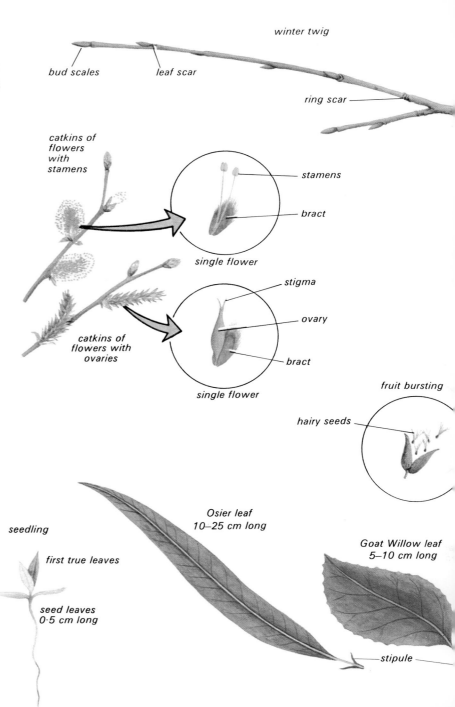

winter twig

bud scales

leaf scar

ring scar

catkins of flowers with stamens

stamens

bract

single flower

stigma

ovary

bract

catkins of flowers with ovaries

single flower

fruit bursting

hairy seeds

seedling

first true leaves

Osier leaf 10–25 cm long

Goat Willow leaf 5–10 cm long

seed leaves 0·5 cm long

stipule

Goat Willow in spring

Scale : 1 cm represents 3 metres

Osier

Goat Willow

cm

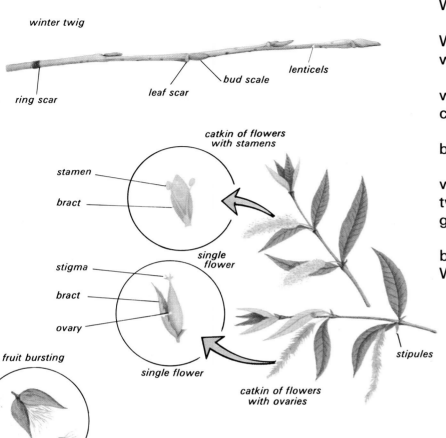

winter twig

ring scar

leaf scar

bud scale

lenticels

catkin of flowers with stamens

stamen

bract

single flower

stigma

bract

ovary

single flower

catkin of flowers with ovaries

stipules

fruit bursting

hairy seeds

White and Crack Willow trees grow in wet woods and by streams.

The wood of one kind of White Willow, which is tough and elastic, is used for making cricket bats.

The Crack Willow is so-called because its branches snap off easily.

All kinds of Willow twigs root easily in water. When the roots are well grown, the twigs may be planted in pots of soil or in the garden.

The illustrations show the difference between the leaves of White and Crack Willow trees.

*ack Willow leaf
·5–4 cm long*

*White Willow leaf
5–10 cm long*

seedling

first true leaves

*seed leaves
0·5 cm long*

Crack Willow in spring

Scale : 1 cm represents 3 metres

White Willow   Crack Willow

cm

54   ASH (*Oleaceae*)

Ash trees grow in woods and hedges; the leaves were once used in large quantities for fodder. The wood, which is strong and elastic, was used for making wooden framed aeroplanes; it makes good oars and hammer handles. An old rhyme says that

    If the Ash is out before the Oak
    Then you're sure to get a soak.
    If the Oak is out before the Ash
    Then you'll only get a splash.

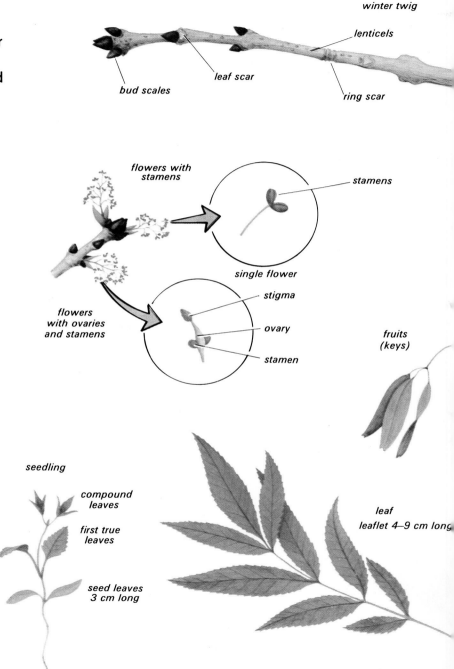

winter twig

lenticels

leaf scar

bud scales

ring scar

flowers with stamens

stamens

single flower

stigma

ovary

stamen

flowers with ovaries and stamens

fruits (keys)

seedling

compound leaves

first true leaves

seed leaves 3 cm long

leaf
leaflet 4–9 cm long

cm

Ash in early summer

Scale : 1 cm represents 3 metres

winter twig

leaf scar

bud scales

lenticels

ring scar

flowers with stamens
and ovaries

petal tube
with ovary inside

sepals

fruits

dead stigmas

dead sepals

burst fruit

winged seed

stamens on
the petals

stigma

sepal

ovary

flower cut open

leaf
4–10 cm long

seeds
rarely
germinate

Lilac trees have been grown in parks and
gardens for a very long time but they rarely
grow wild.

The flowers of the Lilac keep longer if the
leaves are removed from the stems before
they are put into water.

Lilac in spring

Scale : 1 cm represents 3 metres

56   E L D E R (*Caprifoliaceae*)

Elder trees are common in woods and waste places. The seeds germinate easily and, because the seedlings are not eaten by rabbits or other small animals, the plants spread quickly.

Because the pith is so easily removed from the stems it has been used from the times of the Ancient Greeks for making musical pipes; cottagers used the hollow stems as bellows.

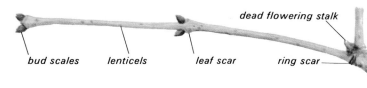

bud scales   *lenticels*   *leaf scar*   *ring scar*   *dead flowering stalk*

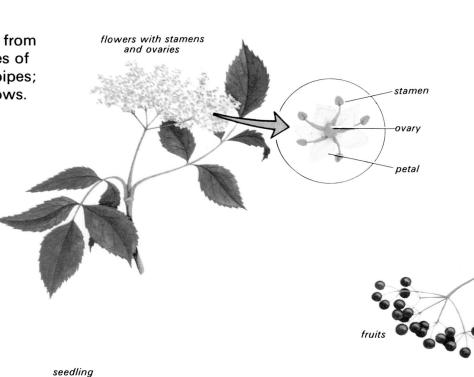

flowers with stamens and ovaries

stamen

ovary

petal

cm

Elder in spring

Scale: 1 cm represents 3 metres

fruits

seedling

compound leaf

first true leaves

seed leaves 1·5 cm long

leaf leaflets 3–7

Strawberry trees are planted in parks. The fruits are not very pleasant to the taste but birds, especially thrushes, eat them when ripe.

Because the fruits take more than a year to ripen, flowers and fruits can be found on the tree at the same time.

flower cut in half

sepal

sepal

ovary

stamen

stigmas

petal tube

sepal

petal tube with stamens and ovary inside

flowers with stamens and ovaries

ring scar

fruits

leaf scar

seedling

first true leaves

seed leaves 0·8cm long

leaf 4–9 cm long

cm

Strawberry tree in spring

Scale : 1 cm represents 3 metres

Spruce trees (Spruce Firs) are grown for their timber in forests, often on mountainsides. The Norway Spruce is grown in plantations to be cut when young and sold as Christmas trees.

Spruce wood is used for telegraph poles and for paper making.

Fir trees, especially the Silver Fir, are planted in parks.

The illustrations show the way the leaves grow on the twigs of the Spruce and the Fir.

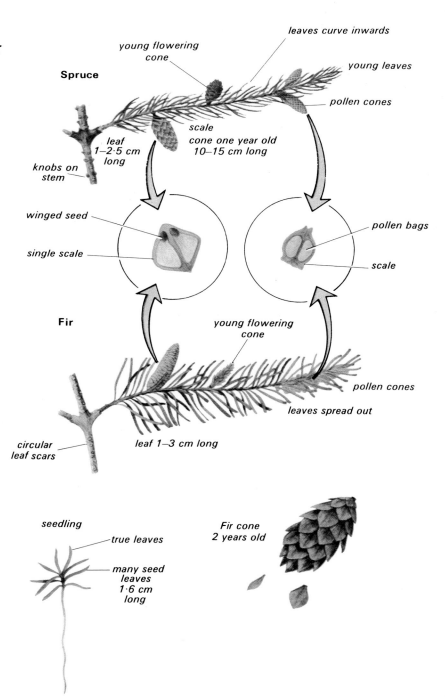

Spruce

young flowering cone

leaves curve inwards

young leaves

pollen cones

scale
cone one year old
10—15 cm long

leaf
1—2.5 cm
long

knobs on
stem

winged seed

single scale

pollen bags

scale

Fir

young flowering cone

pollen cones

leaves spread out

circular
leaf scars

leaf 1—3 cm long

seedling

true leaves

many seed
leaves
1·6 cm
long

Fir cone
2 years old

Norway Spruce in winter

Scale : 1 cm represents 3 metres

cm

Many different kinds of Pine trees are planted in parks. The Scots Pine grows wild in sandy soils and in mountainous places. In summer, cones of four different ages may be seen on the tree: the tiny red flowering cones, small green cones, ripe brown woody cones, and open cones from which the seeds have been blown in dry weather. The cones close up in wet weather.

Squirrels strip the woody scales from the ripe cones.

pollen cones

young flowering cones

young stem with single leaves

needle-leaves in pairs

short shoot

leaf 3–8 cm long

single scale

pollen bags

cone one year old 3–7 cm long

scale

winged seeds

single scale

seedling

open cone 2 years old

true leaves

many seed leaves 2 cm long

winged seed

cm

Scots Pines in autumn

Scale : 1 cm represents 3 metres

60   CEDAR (*Pinaceae*)

Many different kinds of Cedar trees are grown in parks. The most easily recognized is the Cedar of Lebanon, and the largest trees you will see may be more than two hundred years old. Cedar wood is strongly scented.

The wood used for making lead pencils comes from the so-called American Red Cedar (*Juniper virginiana*).

cm

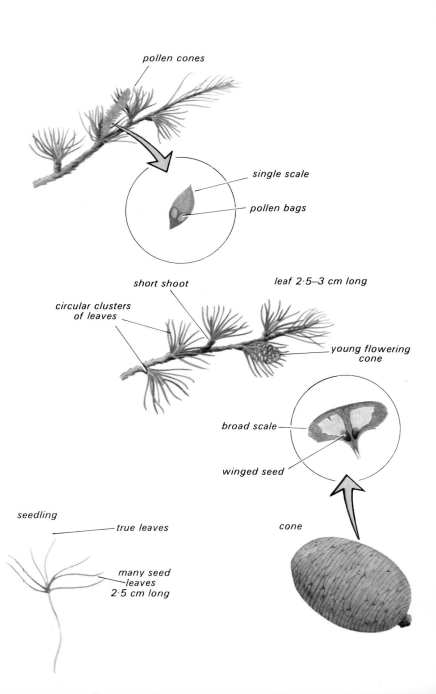

pollen cones

single scale

pollen bags

short shoot

leaf 2·5—3 cm long

circular clusters of leaves

young flowering cone

broad scale

winged seed

cone

seedling

true leaves

many seed leaves 2·5 cm long

Cedar in spring

Scale: 1 cm represents 3 metres

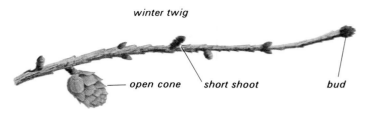

winter twig

— open cone   short shoot   bud

Larch trees are planted in parks, and grown in forestry plantations for their timber which is used for fencing.

Unlike most cone-bearing (conifer) trees they are deciduous (see page 3). Wood wasp larvae (young) spend two or three years tunnelling through the trunks of Larch trees.

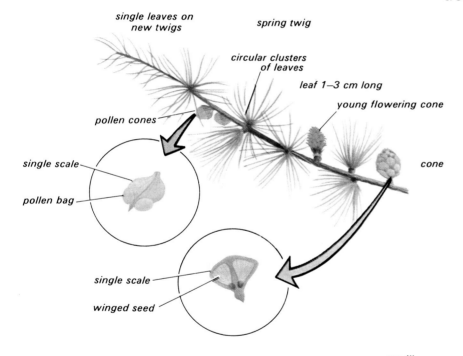

single leaves on new twigs

spring twig

circular clusters of leaves

leaf 1–3 cm long

young flowering cone

pollen cones —

single scale —

pollen bag —

cone

single scale —

winged seed —

seedling

true leaves —

many seed leaves 1·2 cm long —

Larch in spring

Scale : 1 cm represents 3 metres

cm

Many different kinds of Cypress trees are grown in parks. In many varieties their branches spread out from the trunk almost to the ground.

Cypress twigs cannot be seen because they are completely covered by the flattened leaves.

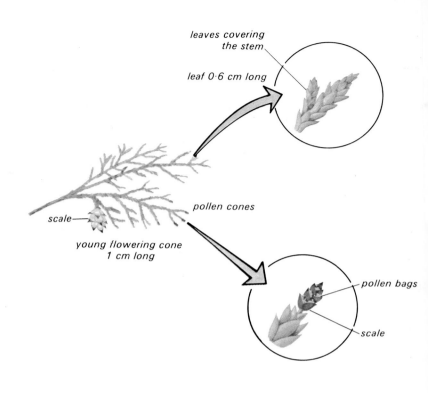

leaves covering the stem

leaf 0·6 cm long

pollen cones

scale

young flowering cone 1 cm long

pollen bags

scale

Cypress in winter

Scale : 1 cm represents 3 metres

seedling of Lawson Cypress

2nd year shoot

first true leaves

seed leaves 0·5 cm long

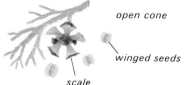

open cone

winged seeds

scale

Yew trees are the longest living trees in Britain. They grow in parks, churchyards, and on chalky hillsides.

The leaves and green seeds are very poisonous to man and other furry animals, but the red juicy case is eaten by thrushes.

The bark of the tree is red and flakes off in patches; posts made from the trunks last longer than iron posts, and long bows used to be made from the branches.

Yew trees are often trimmed into the shapes of animals; this way of cutting trees is called topiary.

one scale

pollen bags

pollen cones

new leaves

seed

case

young seed

flower containing
the seed

leaf
1–3 cm long

case

seed

ripe seed

seedling

true leaves

seed leaves
1·8 cm long

cm

Yew in summer

Scale : 1 cm represents 3 metres

64   Bibliography

Allen, G. and Denslow, J., *Flowers* (Clue Books, Oxford University Press)
Edlin, H. L., *British Woodland Trees* (Batsford)
Hadfield, M., *British Trees. A Guide for Everyman* (Dent)
Harrison, S. G., *Garden Shrubs and Trees* (Kew Series, Eyre and Spottiswood)
Holbrook, A. W., *Pocket Guide to Trees in Britain* (Country Life)
McClintock and Fitter, *Guide to Wild Flowers* (Collins)
Step, *Wayside and Woodland Trees* (Warne)
Whitehead, *The Book of Flowering Trees and Shrubs* (Warne)

The photograph on page 55 is reproduced by courtesy of the Royal Forestry Society of England, Wales and Northern Ireland.

Index